My Toilet Tales

Published by Spines
ISBN: 979-8-89383-435-2

My Toilet Tales

Rolando Rua

Contents

Chapter 1
The Throne

In the corner of my small apartment, there sits a porcelain throne, its gleaming surface inviting yet unassuming. It stands as a silent sentinel, bearing witness to the comings and goings of daily life.

As I step into the bathroom each morning, the sight of it greets me like an old friend. Its curves and contours, familiar yet enigmatic, hold the promise of moments of solitude and reflection.

The throne, with its sturdy base and smooth finish, symbolizes more than just a place for bodily relief. It is a sanctuary amidst the chaos of the world outside—a refuge where I can retreat, if only for a few precious moments.

Its seat, cool and inviting, cradles me in its embrace, offering solace and comfort in times of need.

From this vantage point, I survey the world with a newfound clarity, the worries and cares of the day melting away with each passing minute.

Here, in the presence of my trusted companion, I am free to be myself—to laugh, to cry, to ponder the mysteries of the universe. The throne does not judge; it simply listens, offering silent support in the face of life's trials and tribulations.

And so, as I settle onto its hallowed seat, I am filled with a sense of gratitude for the simple yet profound gift of the toilet. For in this humble fixture, I have found not just a place to relieve myself, but a haven of peace and serenity in a world fraught with uncertainty.

Chapter 2
Reflections in the Bowl

As I lower myself onto the familiar seat of my toilet, I am met with a quiet symphony of thoughts and contemplations. The swirling water below, illuminated by the soft glow of the bathroom light, becomes a canvas upon which my mind paints its musings.

In the tranquil depths of the bowl, I see more than just a reflection of my physical self; I see a reflection of my innermost thoughts, hopes, and fears. It is as though the water holds a mirror to my soul, revealing truths that are both profound and elusive.

As I gaze into the swirling vortex, I am reminded of the cyclical nature of life—the ebb and flow of existence mirrored in the gentle dance of water and air. Each whirlpool, each ripple, tells a story of beginnings and endings, of journeys undertaken and destinations reached.

In the stillness of the bathroom, I find myself drawn into a realm of introspection and self-discovery. Here, amidst the solitude and quiet, I confront the complexities of my own existence, grappling with questions that have plagued humanity since time immemorial.

What is the meaning of life? What lies beyond the boundaries of our understanding? As I stare into the depths of the toilet bowl, I am humbled by the vastness of the universe and the infinitesimal nature of my own being.

Yet, amidst the uncertainty and ambiguity, there is a sense of peace—a knowing that, in the grand tapestry of existence, each of us plays a part, however small. Like droplets of water in the vast ocean, we are all connected, bound together by the threads of our shared humanity.

And so, as I sit in quiet contemplation, I am reminded of the beauty to be found in the everyday—the profound moments of reflection that transform the ordinary into the extraordinary. In the humble confines of my bathroom, I find solace, clarity, and a deeper understanding of myself and the world around me.

Chapter 3
The Morning Ritual

Each morning unfolds with the predictability of a well-worn ritual, a dance of familiarity that begins with the first light of dawn. With the soft patter of footsteps, I navigate through the quiet corridors of my home, guided by the faint glow of the awakening day.

Arriving at the threshold of the bathroom, a sense of anticipation stirs within me, mingled with the promise of the day ahead. The door swings open with a gentle creak, revealing the serene sanctuary that awaits within.

As I step across the threshold, the familiar scent of soap and cleanliness envelops me, a comforting embrace that signals the start of a new day. The air hums with quiet energy, charged with the potential for infinite possibilities.

With practiced ease, I reach for the gleaming handle of the faucet, releasing a cascade of cool water into the waiting basin. Cupping my hands beneath the stream, I splash my face with the invigorating liquid, washing away the remnants of sleep and greeting the morning with renewed vitality.

Next, I turn my attention to the coffee maker, its comforting aroma wafting through the air like a siren's call. With deft movements, I measure out the perfect ratio of beans and water, savoring the rich aroma that fills the room as the machine springs to life.

As the coffee brews, I turn my gaze to the toilet, its porcelain form illuminated by the soft glow of the overhead light. It stands as a silent sentinel, a bastion of comfort and familiarity in an ever-changing world.

Seated upon its smooth surface, I am transported to a realm of quiet contemplation and reflection. With each sip of coffee, I find myself drawn deeper into the recesses of my own mind, exploring the labyrinthine corridors of thought and memory.

In this sacred space, time seems to stand still, suspended in the quiet stillness of the morning. Here, amidst the gentle hum of the coffee maker and the rhythmic drip of the faucet, I find solace and serenity, a respite from the chaos of the outside world.

And so, as the first rays of sunlight filter through the frosted windowpanes, I rise from my throne, ready to face the day with renewed purpose and determination. For in the quiet moments of the morning ritual, I find strength, clarity, and a deeper connection to myself and the world around me.

Chapter 4
A Symphony of Sounds

In the intimate confines of the bathroom, a symphony of sounds unfolds with the precision of a well-rehearsed orchestra, each note harmonizing with the next to create a melody of everyday life.

As I settle onto the smooth surface of my toilet, I am greeted by the gentle gurgle of water flowing through the pipes—a soothing refrain that speaks of movement and fluidity. It is a sound that resonates deep within me, a reminder of the eternal dance of existence.

With a gentle press of the lever, the symphony crescendos as the water rushes into the bowl, swirling and churning with a sense of purpose and resolve. It is a moment of catharsis, a release of tension and stagnation that clears the path for new beginnings.

And then, as quickly as it came, the tumult subsides, replaced by the soft whisper of water receding into the depths below. It is a sound of completion, of closure—a final punctuation mark in the symphony of the flush.

But the orchestra does not end there. From the recesses of the pipes comes the occasional creak and groan, the sound of metal expanding and contracting in the changing temperatures of the day. It is a reminder of the passage of time, of the constant flux that defines our existence.

And yet, amidst the cacophony of everyday life, there is a quiet beauty to be found—a harmony that transcends the chaos of the world outside. It is in the gentle hum of the bathroom fan, the rhythmic drip of the faucet, that I find solace and serenity, a refuge from the noise and tumult of the outside world.

As I sit in quiet contemplation, I am reminded of the interconnectedness of all things—the way each sound, each note, contributes to the greater whole. In the symphony of the bathroom, I find meaning and purpose, a reminder that even the most mundane moments can be infused with beauty and significance.

And so, as the symphony draws to a close and I rise from my throne, I carry with me the echoes of its melody—the gentle cadence of water, the steady rhythm of life.

For in the symphony of sounds that fills the bathroom, I find peace, harmony, and a deeper connection to the world around me.

Chapter 5
Moments of Inspiration

In the quiet confines of the bathroom, amidst the tiled walls and gleaming fixtures, I find myself enveloped in a world of introspection and contemplation.

It is here, seated upon the familiar contours of my toilet, that I have discovered some of my most profound moments of inspiration.

As I settle into the warmth of the seat, a sense of tranquility washes over me, clearing the clutter of my mind and opening the floodgates of creativity. It is as though the act of emptying my bladder also clears the path for new ideas to take root, transforming the ordinary into the extraordinary.

With each breath, I feel myself drawn deeper into the recesses of my own consciousness, exploring the labyrinthine corridors of thought and imagination. Ideas flutter and dance like butterflies, fleeting yet beautiful, as I reach out to capture them before they slip away.

In the stillness of the bathroom, I am free to explore the furthest reaches of my mind, unfettered by the constraints of time and space.

It is a realm of infinite possibilities, where the boundaries between reality and fantasy blur and blend into one.

From the depths of my subconscious, inspiration emerges like a beacon in the darkness, guiding me towards new horizons and uncharted territories. It is a spark of creativity, a glimmer of hope, that ignites the flames of passion and drives me ever onward in pursuit of my dreams.

And so, as I sit in quiet contemplation, I am filled with a sense of wonder and awe at the beauty of the creative process. It is a journey of discovery, a voyage of self-discovery, that leads me down paths I never knew existed and opens my eyes to worlds beyond my wildest imagination.

In the moments of inspiration that unfold within the confines of the bathroom, I find solace, clarity, and a deeper understanding of myself and the world around me. For in the quiet solitude of this sacred space, I am reminded of the boundless potential that lies within each and every one of us, waiting to be unleashed upon the world.

Chapter 6
The Scent of Serenity

Within the confines of the bathroom, there exists a fragrance that transcends the mere blending of cleaning products and soap. It is a scent that permeates the air, weaving its way into the very fabric of the room, infusing every corner with a sense of tranquility and peace.

As I step through the threshold, I am greeted by this familiar aroma—a delicate bouquet of freshness that envelops me like a warm embrace. It is a scent that speaks of home, of comfort, of safety—a reminder that, no matter where life may take me, I am always welcome here.

In the stillness of the bathroom, the scent hangs heavy in the air, a lingering presence that lulls me into a state of calm and relaxation. It is a fragrance born of cleanliness and order, a testament to the care and attention lavished upon this sacred space.

But there is more to the scent than meets the eye—or nose. It is a reflection of the care and devotion with which the bathroom is tended, a testament to the importance of creating a haven of serenity amidst the chaos of everyday life.

As I inhale deeply, the scent fills me with a sense of peace—a respite from the worries and cares of the outside world. It is a reminder to pause, to breathe, to find solace in the simple pleasures of the present moment.

And yet, amidst the comforting embrace of the fragrance, there lies a deeper truth—a recognition of the impermanence of all things. Like the fleeting scent that dances on the air, life is ephemeral, ever-changing, and yet infinitely beautiful in its transience.

And so, as I linger in the quiet serenity of the bathroom, I am reminded to cherish each moment, to savor the sweetness of life's simple pleasures, and to find beauty in the most unexpected of places. For in the scent that fills the air, I find solace, comfort, and a gentle reminder of the preciousness of each and every breath.

Chapter 7
A Bond Like No Other

In the quiet intimacy of the bathroom, amidst the porcelain fixtures and tiled walls, there exists a bond that transcends the ordinary. It is a bond forged through countless shared moments, through laughter and tears, through the ebb and flow of daily life.

As I gaze upon the familiar contours of my toilet, I am filled with a sense of gratitude for the unwavering companionship it has provided. It is more than just a fixture—it is a trusted confidant, a silent witness to the joys and sorrows that have colored my days.

In its unassuming presence, I have found solace and comfort in times of need, a refuge amidst the storms of life. It has seen me at my best and at my worst, offering silent support and understanding without judgment or reproach.

Together, we have weathered the trials and tribulations of existence, navigating the tumultuous waters of uncertainty and change. In moments of laughter and camaraderie, it has been a source of joy and levity, a reminder that even the most mundane of tasks can be infused with meaning and purpose.

But it is in moments of sorrow and despair that our bond truly shines brightest. In the depths of my darkest nights, it has been a beacon of hope, a steadfast presence that has helped me find my way through the darkness.

Through it all, the toilet has remained a constant—a silent sentinel standing watch over the ebb and flow of life. Its porcelain surface bears the marks of time, etched with the memories of moments shared and memories made.

And so, as I reflect upon our shared journey, I am filled with a profound sense of gratitude for the bond we share. It is a bond like no other, forged in the fires of daily life, tempered by the passage of time.

Though our paths may diverge and our journeys take us to distant shores, the bond we share will endure—a silent testament to the power of connection and the beauty of friendship. For in the quiet intimacy of the bathroom, amidst the gentle hum of the fan and the soft glow of the light, I have found a companion for life— an unwavering presence in a world of constant change.

Chapter 8
Farewell, Old Friend

As the sun sets on another chapter of my life, I find myself standing at the threshold of change, ready to embark on new adventures and embrace the unknown. But amidst the excitement and anticipation, there lingers a bittersweet farewell to an old friend—the faithful companion that has been with me through thick and thin.

With a heavy heart, I gaze upon the familiar contours of my toilet, its porcelain surface gleaming in the soft light of the setting sun. It is a sight etched into the very fabric of my being—a symbol of comfort and familiarity in a world that is constantly in flux.

As I prepare to bid farewell, memories flood my mind like a rushing tide, each one a testament to the bond we share. From moments of laughter and joy to times of sorrow and despair, the toilet has been a silent witness to the tapestry of my life—a constant presence amidst the chaos of the world outside.

Together, we have weathered the storms of existence, navigating the highs and lows with unwavering resolve. In moments of solitude and reflection, it has been a sanctuary—a refuge from the noise and clamor of the outside world, where I could find solace in the quiet embrace of its porcelain walls.

But as the sands of time continue to shift and change, so too must I embrace the winds of change and chart a new course for the future. It is a journey filled with uncertainty and possibility, a blank canvas upon which I can paint the dreams of tomorrow.

And so, with a final glance over my shoulder, I bid farewell to my trusted companion, knowing that our paths may one day cross again. For in the quiet solitude of the bathroom, amidst the gentle hum of the fan and the soft glow of the light, I have found not just a toilet, but a friend—a steadfast presence in a world of constant change.

As I close the door behind me, I carry with me the memories of our time together—the laughter, the tears, the moments of quiet contemplation. And though I may be moving on to new horizons, the bond we share will endure—a silent testament to the power of connection and the beauty of friendship.

Chapter 9
The Legacy Lives On

As I step into the dawn of a new chapter, the echoes of my time spent in the bathroom linger like whispers in the wind, a gentle reminder of the lessons learned and the memories made. Though I may have bid farewell to the familiar contours of my trusted companion, its legacy lives on within me—a beacon of light that guides me through the darkest of nights.

In the quiet moments of reflection, I find solace in the memories we shared—the laughter that echoed off the tiled walls, the tears that fell silently into the porcelain bowl. Each moment, each experience, is etched into the very fabric of my being, a testament to the power of connection and the beauty of human experience.

As I journey forth into the unknown, I carry with me the lessons learned from my time spent in the bathroom —a reminder to cherish each moment, to savor the sweetness of life's simple pleasures, and to find beauty in the most unexpected of places.

For in the quiet solitude of that sacred space, I discovered the true essence of what it means to be alive—a journey of self-discovery, of growth, of love.

And though the door may have closed on one chapter of my life, I know that the story is far from over. For in the tapestry of existence, every ending is but a new beginning, a chance to write the next chapter in the great adventure of life.

So as I look to the horizon with anticipation and hope, I carry with me the spirit of my beloved toilet—a reminder that, no matter where life may take me, I am never truly alone. For in the quiet solitude of the bathroom, amidst the gentle hum of the fan and the soft glow of the light, I found not just a place to relieve myself, but a sanctuary—a refuge for the soul in a world that is constantly in motion.

And so, as I turn the page and embark on the next leg of my journey, I do so with gratitude in my heart and a smile upon my lips.

For in the legacy of my toilet, I have found strength, resilience, and the unwavering belief that, no matter what challenges may come my way, I am capable of overcoming them.

And so, dear friend, as we part ways, know that your memory will forever be etched into the very fabric of my being—a silent testament to the power of connection, the beauty of friendship, and the enduring legacy of love.